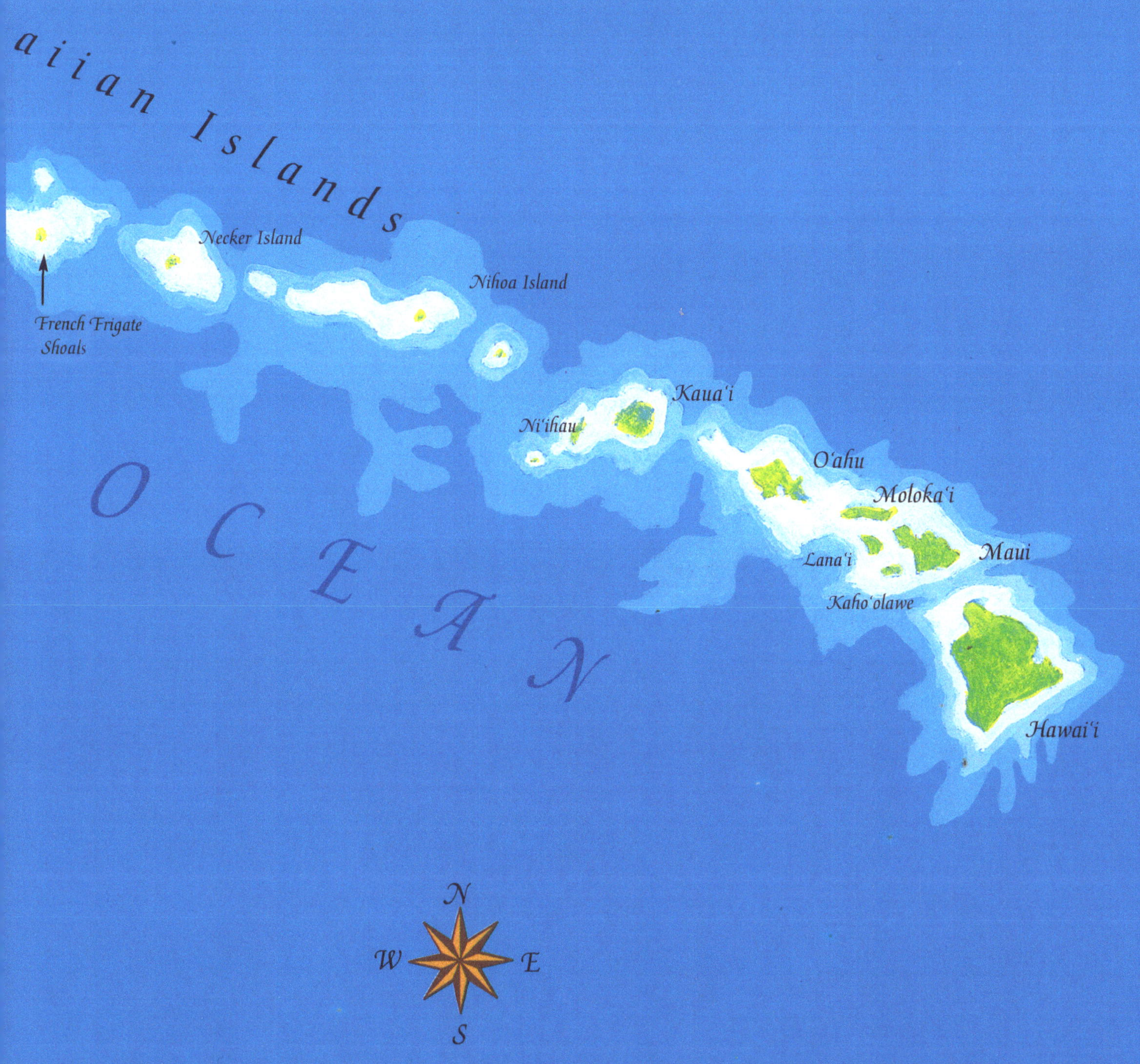
aiian Islands
Necker Island
Nihoa Island
French Frigate Shoals
Kaua'i
Ni'ihau
O'ahu
Moloka'i
Maui
Lana'i
Kaho'olawe
Hawai'i
OCEAN
N
W
E
S

DISCOVER HAWAI'I'S SOARING SEABIRDS

Written & Illustrated by Katherine Orr

Originally published by

ISLAND HERITAGE
PUBLISHING

Reprinted in 2020 by Katherine Orr
with permission from Island Heritage.
For educational use.
Please address orders and correspondence to:

Katherine Orr
44-119 Bayview Haven Place
Kaneohe, HI, 96744, USA
(808) 234-5508; www.katherineshelleyorr.com

Copyright © 2020 by Katherine S. Orr
All rights reserved. Portions of this book may
be reproduced and modified for educational
purposes with permission from the author.
Printed in the USA

DISCOVER Hawai'i's SOARING Seabirds

Written and Illustrated by Katherine Orr

CONTENTS

Introduction 3
Seabirds of Hawai'i 4
Designed for Life at Sea 6
Albatrosses 8
    Black-footed Albatross 10
    Laysan Albatross, or *Mōlī* 12
Petrels and Shearwaters 14
    Dark-rumped Petrel or *'Ua'u* 16
    Bonin Petrel 17
    Bulwer's Petrel or *'Ou* 17
    Wedge-tailed Shearwater, or *'Ua'u kani* ... 18
    Christmas Shearwater 19
    Newell's Shearwater, or *'A'o* 20
Storm-Petrels 22
    Band-rumped Storm-Petrel or *'Akē'akē* ... 23
    Sooty Storm-Petrel 23
Tropicbirds 24
    White-tailed Tropicbird, or *Koa'e kea* ... 25
    Red-tailed Tropicbird, or *Koa'e 'ula* 25
Boobies 26
    Brown Booby, or *'Ā* 28
    Red-footed Booby, or *'Ā* 28
    Masked Booby, or *'Ā* 29
Frigatebirds 30
    Great Frigatebird, or *'Iwa* 31
Terns and Noddies 32
    Sooty Tern, or *'Ewa'ewa* 33
    Gray-backed Tern, or *Pakalakala* 34
    White Tern, or *Manu-O-Kū* 35
    Black Noddy, or *Noio* 36
    Brown Noddy, or *Noio Kōhā* 37
    Blue-gray Noddy 37
Surviving the Heat 38
Other Dangers 40
The Future of Seabirds 42
How You Can Help 43
Glossary 44
Index 45

INTRODUCTION

Pink and gold colors reflect across the waves as the sun sinks over the ocean. Offshore, a flock of sooty terns chatters noisily as the birds swoop and dive at small fish below the water's surface. A red-footed booby glides low over the sea, heading towards land. Seemingly from nowhere, a great frigatebird rushes up behind the booby. The booby tries to escape by turning one way and then another, but the frigatebird twists and turns like a dancer in the sky, keeping close to the booby all the while. Soon, the booby is so upset that it regurgitates a fish. This is just what the frigatebird wanted; it catches the fish in mid-air and quickly swallows it. Mission accomplished, the frigatebird flies off and the booby continues on its way to shore where it will join other boobies to sleep for the night.

Sooty terns, red-footed boobies, and great frigatebirds are some of Hawai'i's many seabirds. Twenty-two species of seabird nest in Hawai'i, but the sea is their true home. At sea they find their food and spend most of their days. While some birds, like the red-footed boobies, return to land each night to sleep, others, like the sooty terns, spend many months, even years, at sea and only come ashore to hatch and raise their young. This book introduces you to these special birds which form a living link between Hawai'i's land and the vast surrounding sea.

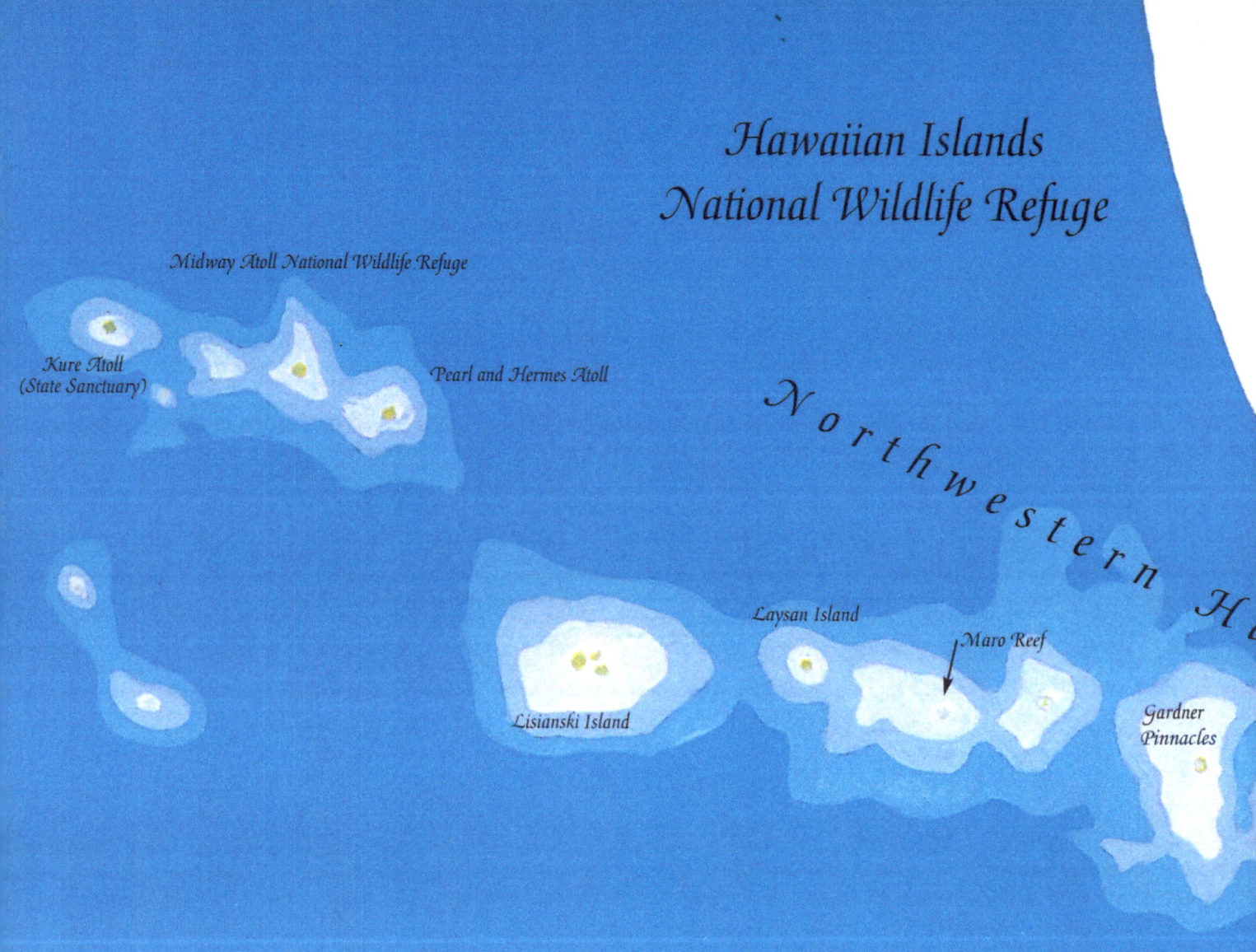

SEABIRDS OF HAWAI'I

Some scientists say that more than twelve million seabirds nest in the Hawaiian Islands. Most of these birds nest in the Northwestern Hawaiian Islands, also called the Northwest Chain, or the Leeward Islands. Except for Kure and Midway, these low, dry, islands are part of the **Hawaiian Islands National Wildlife Refuge**. One of the purposes of the Hawaiian Islands National Wildlife Refuge is to protect seabirds. Nobody lives on these islands, and people must receive special permission to visit them. At one time, many seabirds also nested throughout Hawai'i's main islands, but human activities and the animals people brought with them caused the birds nesting on these islands to die out. Pigs, cats, dogs, rats, and mongooses - all brought to Hawai'i by people - eat seabird eggs and chicks, and have caused many groups of ground-nesting seabirds to disappear completely from some Hawaiian islands.

Small islands off of the main islands, such as Moku Manu and Manana off O'ahu, and Ka'ula off Ni'ihau, are also important nesting areas for Hawai'i's seabirds. Because these tiny islands are so close to human activities, the birds that nest here need protection from human disturbance.

Most seabirds wander great distances across the ocean when they are young, and only return to land when it is time for them to nest. Often, this is not until they are five or more years old. All seabirds are born on land, and while most of them return to nest in the place of their birth, a few young birds may choose a new land for their nests. In this way, seabirds from other places first came to Hawai'i.

Most of Hawai'i's seabirds nest together in groups called *colonies*. Because there is so little land to nest on compared to the huge expanse of ocean where the birds live and feed throughout most of their lives, nesting in colonies allows a large number of birds to nest in a small amount of space. By nesting together in colonies at different times of year, the same space can be used more than once by different species of seabirds. Nearly all of Hawai'i's seabird species nest in other parts of the Pacific as well. The Newell's shearwater, however, nests nowhere else in the world.

DESIGNED FOR LIFE AT SEA

Because their home is the sea, seabirds are different from land birds in some important ways. Water-repellent feathers help keep them dry, and their long, slim, pointed wings are designed for many hours, weeks, even months, of flying. Sooty terns are amazing fliers. Once sooty terns learn to fly, they live in the air for about five years. If they sit on the ocean at all it is only briefly, perhaps because their feathers are not sufficiently waterproof. The feathers of all seabirds repel water because of a waxy substance produced by a gland at the base of the tail. The birds use their bills to spread the wax on their

Sooty tern

A straight bill helps the booby dive after its food.

A hooked bill helps the Frigatebird snatch fish from the ocean surface.

feathers.

Because seabirds drink saltwater, their bodies need a way to get rid of the extra salt. Special glands near the eyes remove salt through the nostrils of most seabirds. Some birds let this very salty water drip off the tip of the bill, while others shake their heads or blow it out their noses.

Most seabirds have webbed feet which help them paddle on the surface of the ocean. Albatrosses also use their webbed feet to help them take flight. Boobies, shearwaters, and tropicbirds use their webbed feet to chase fish and squid underwater. The legs of shearwaters and tropicbirds are set far back on the body to help them swim fast underwater. In fact, their legs are set so far back that tropicbirds cannot walk. They move about by pushing the body forward with their legs.

Often, seabirds must travel far between their food supply at sea and the chick they are feeding on land. Most seabirds swallow the food they catch for their chicks. In this way they don't have to carry food in their bills for long distances and they can eat enough to feed themselves and their chicks. Back at the nest, the parent brings the food up from its stomach and feeds the chick from its mouth.

Some years there is a greater food supply than other years. Seabird chicks grow more quickly when they have plenty to eat, and grow more slowly when they have less food.

Red-tailed tropicbirds

Laysan albatross feeding its chick.

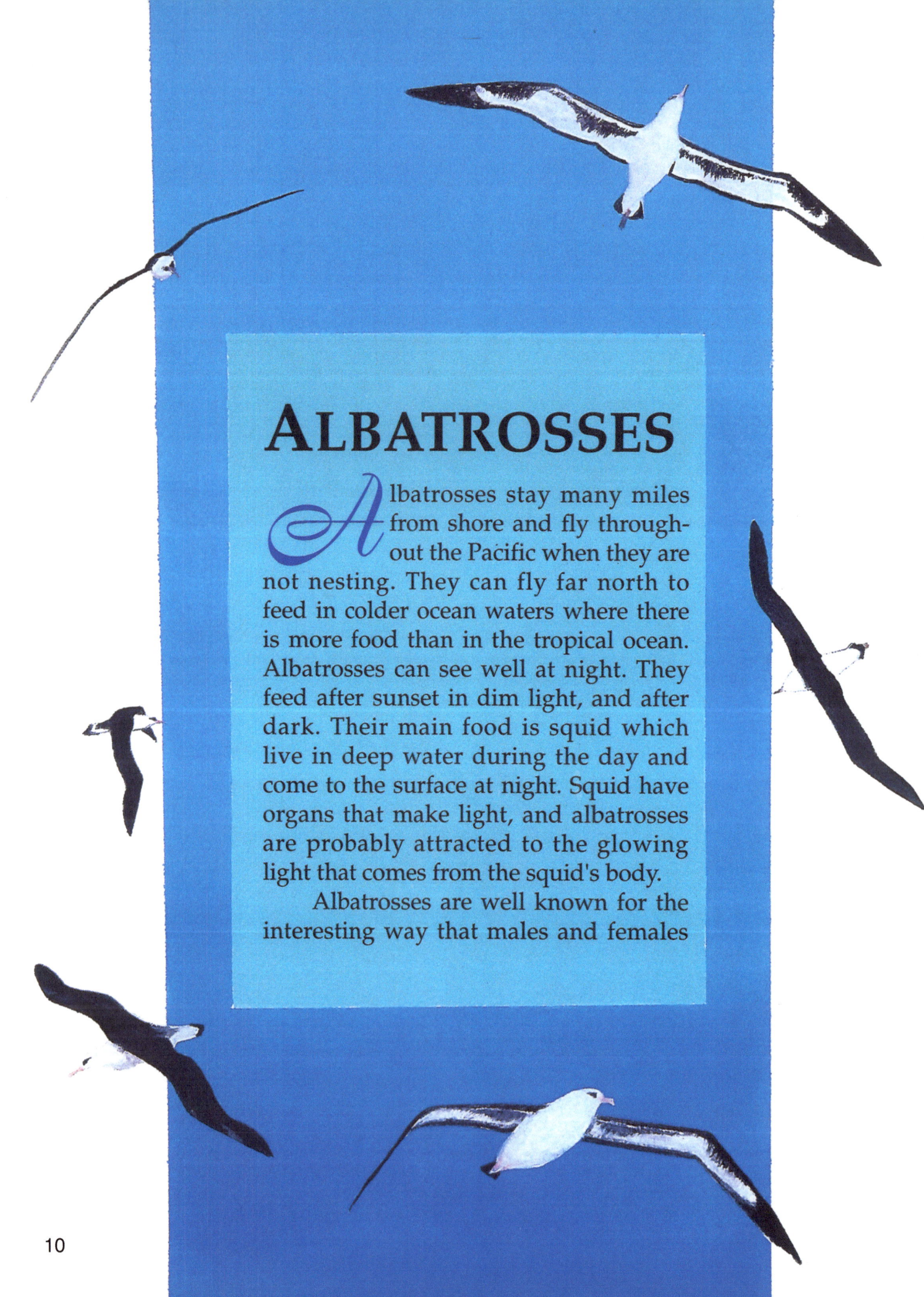

ALBATROSSES

Albatrosses stay many miles from shore and fly throughout the Pacific when they are not nesting. They can fly far north to feed in colder ocean waters where there is more food than in the tropical ocean. Albatrosses can see well at night. They feed after sunset in dim light, and after dark. Their main food is squid which live in deep water during the day and come to the surface at night. Squid have organs that make light, and albatrosses are probably attracted to the glowing light that comes from the squid's body.

Albatrosses are well known for the interesting way that males and females

Laysan albatrosses courting each other.

court, or attract each other as mates. During courtship, the birds stand facing each other while making a fantastic display of sounds and movements. They bob their heads up and down, make cow-like "mooing" noises as they point their bills to the sky, clap their bills like chattering teeth, whinny like horses, shake their heads, and raise their wings while nibbling themselves under the wing in the "armpit" area. Usually only young birds looking for a mate court each other in these wonderful ways. Once two birds accept each other as mates, they remain together for life. Although they will go their separate ways out on the ocean, when nesting season arrives they will find each other and nest at the same spot year after year.

The Laysan albatross and the black-footed albatross both nest in the Hawaiian Islands. With a distance of more than 2 meters (about 6 feet) between the tips of their outstretched wings, these albatrosses are the largest seabirds in the northern Pacific Ocean.

A third albatross - the short-tailed albatross - sometimes lands in Hawai'i, and nests are occasionally found on Midway Island. In the last two hundred years, many colonies of short-tailed albatrosses, as well as Laysan and black-footed albatrosses, were destroyed by people who killed them and sold their feathers. In the 1980's, scientists believed there were only about 400 short-tailed albatrosses left on earth. Today their numbers are growing, but short-tailed albatrosses are still considered to be in danger of becoming *extinct* - of disappearing from the earth forever.

BLACK-FOOTED ALBATROSS

Black-footed albatrosses are found throughout the North Pacific Ocean, but most of them breed in the Northwestern Hawaiian Islands. They are often seen following ships at sea, eating the ship's garbage that has been thrown overboard. They are sometimes seen from the main islands, soaring low across the waves.

Black-footed albatrosses are dark grayish-brown all over the body with

Short-tailed albatross

a white patch behind each eye and some white at the base of the bill. They have grayish-black legs, feet, and bills. Black-footed albatrosses are slightly larger and heavier than Laysan albatrosses, and have a slightly larger wingspan. Most of Hawai'i's black footed albatrosses begin arriving on land to breed in late October. Their favorite nesting areas are open sandy ground near shore where the wind blows strongly. Their nests are nothing more than a hollow area scraped in the sand with a rim of packed sand around it. The male and female build the nest together. They sometimes add twigs and leaves to the rim.

The parents take turns incubating the single white egg and guarding the chick until it is about three weeks old. For the first few days, the parents feed their chick a fishy-smelling oil from their stomachs. After that, the chick is fed mainly squid. At first the chick is fed every day, but feedings become less frequent as the chick grows older.

Most black-footed albatross chicks are ready to fly in less than five months. Generally, the chicks leave the nesting area in late June. They will live at sea and not return to breed until they are at least five years old, although birds as young as one year old come to dance and look for mates.

Albatrosses cannot take flight from the ground or the ocean without the help of a strong breeze.

Black-footed albatross

LAYSAN ALBATROSS OR MŌLĪ

The Laysan albatross has a white body with a gray-black back, tail, and wings. The undersides of the wings have some white along the center, and there is a black patch in front of each eye, fading to gray on the cheeks. The bill, legs, and feet are pinkish-gray.

Laysan albatrosses nest mainly in the Northwestern Hawaiian Islands, but nesting colonies are also found on Niʻihau, Moku Manu and Kaʻena Point, Oʻahu, and Kauaʻi.

Laysan albatrosses begin coming ashore to find a mate when they are about three years old but they do not nest until they are at least five. Most Laysan albatrosses do not start to nest until they are eight or nine years old. They are known to live as long as 42 years.

The nesting season for Laysan albatrosses begins in early November. Adults place their nests in grassy, open areas, often below shrubs or trees. The nest sites are usually near windward bluffs or cliffs where there is a steady wind so the birds can take flight. Laysan albatrosses are usually gentle and are not afraid of people unless approached too closely. On Kauaʻi, they can be found nesting near shrubs alongside people's houses.

Males and females build the nest by taking turns scraping out a hollow on the ground. They sit in the hollow and scrape together sand and leaves

Laysan Albatross talks to its egg.

Newly hatched chick

Growing chick

Feathers have replaced most of the down.

As the albatross chick grows, its covering of down is replaced by feathers.

with their bills, forming a rim around the hollow. The female lays a single white egg, usually in late November. The male and female take turns sitting on the egg until it hatches after about sixty-four days. The chick begins to make peeping sounds while it is still in the egg, and the parents "talk" to it in high squeaks. Hatching is difficult for albatross chicks - it may take two to six days to get free of the egg.

Laysan albatross chicks remain in or near the nest for about five and a half months. As the chicks grow older, their parents spend more time at sea, returning only to feed the chicks. By August, the young birds have left the nest for the open ocean, and no Laysan albatrosses come to land until the following November when nesting season starts again.

PETRELS AND SHEARWATERS

Three species of petrel and three species of shearwater nest in the Hawaiian Islands. Petrels and Shearwaters are medium-sized birds with long, pointed wings that help them soar over the ocean, and hooked bills that help them grab their prey. Along with albatrosses and storm-petrels, petrels and shearwaters have nostrils that form small tubes, giving this group of birds the name "tubenoses."

Petrels see well at night and usually feed in dim light and darkness. They spot their food from the air and dip into the water while flying, or land on the surface for a short time as they grab their prey. Shearwaters don't see very well at night, so they usually feed during the day. They often chase after small fish underwater, paddling with their webbed feet and wings.

Both petrels and shearwaters have a very good sense of smell which they use to find food, and probably also use to find their nesting burrows.

Hawaiian petrels and shearwaters return to their nesting colonies at night. They begin arriving on land just after sunset and head for sea just before sunrise. Males and females often remain paired for life, and return

year after year to the island where they were hatched.

Most petrels and shearwaters dig burrows, or tunnels, to nest in. Sometimes they use the same nesting burrow again and again. The female lays a single egg at the far end of the burrow, and both parents take turns incubating the egg. The parents feed the chick oil, fish, and squid from their own stomachs. At first, the chick is fed nearly every night, but as the chick grows older it is fed less often. After awhile, the chick weighs more than its parents, but as its feathers grow in and as it exercises its wing muscles, the chick loses the extra weight. When the chick is ready, it leaves the colony at night, flying alone to sea where it will spend most of its life.

Petrels and shearwaters are naturally attracted to lights. This might be because some of their foods - squid and other sea animals - make light with their bodies. The birds probably find food by flying to the light coming from these animals. For those shearwaters and petrels that nest along the shore, or in the Northwestern Hawaiian Islands, this attraction to lights is not a problem. But for Newell's shearwaters and dark-rumped petrels that must fly over towns and highways at night on their way between sea and mountains, the attraction to lights causes many injuries and deaths.

Dark-rumped Petrel

DARK-RUMPED PETREL, OR ʻUAʻU

The dark-rumped petrel is white below and dark gray above with a white forehead. It nests only in Hawaiʻi and in the Galapagos Islands, off Ecuador. Although dark-rumped petrels once nested in the mountains of many Hawaiian Islands, the arrival of people and animals such as rats and mongooses have caused these birds to disappear from most of the islands. In ancient times, the Hawaiians ate dark-rumped petrels. The young birds were a valued food that was said to be prized by royalty. Scientists have found nesting colonies of dark-rumped petrels in Haleakalā Crater on Maui, and high in the mountains on Hawaiʻi and the north shore of Kauaʻi. A few dark-rumped petrels are believed to be nesting on Lanaʻi and Molokaʻi.

Dark-rumped petrels dig burrows that may be several meters long. The female lays a single egg, usually in early May. The chicks hatch in July and August. Young dark-rumped petrels leave their burrows and fly to sea at night in late October and early November. In areas where they must fly past power lines or many lights, some young birds are injured or killed each year on their first trip to sea.

BONIN PETREL

Bonin petrels are dark gray on the head, back, and tail. The forehead, neck, breast, and belly are white. The undersides of the wings are white with dark edges.

Bonin petrels breed in the Northwestern Hawaiian Islands. Adult birds arrive at their breeding colony in August, but the female doesn't lay her egg until January, February, or March. The adults dig burrows in the sand that are up to 3 meters (almost 10 feet) long. Most eggs hatch in March and April, and most of the young petrels leave their burrows and fly to sea in late May through June.

Bonin Petrel

BULWER'S PETREL OR 'OU

Bulwer's petrels are dark gray-brown with pale bars on the upper sides of the wings. They breed on several island groups in the Pacific Ocean, including the Hawaiian Islands. Bulwer's petrels nest on many of the small islands off the main islands, as well as the Northwestern Hawaiian Islands.

Most adults return to their nesting sites in April. They nest in holes and rock crevices, or under shrubs and rock ledges. The egg is usually laid in late May or June. Most chicks hatch in July and August, and are ready to leave the nest and head to sea in September.

Bulwer's Petrel

19

Wedge-tailed Shearwaters

WEDGE-TAILED SHEARWATER OR *UA'U-KANI*

Wedge-tailed shearwaters nest on many of the Hawaiian Islands as well as throughout other parts of the Pacific and Indian Oceans. They are the largest Hawaiian shearwater, with dark gray-brown on the head, back, tail, and wings, and lighter feathers on the belly, breast, and throat. A few of the wedge-tailed shearwaters in Hawai'i are dark gray-brown all over. The bill is gray-black and the legs and feet are pinkish. They can be recognized in flight by the long, wedge-shaped tail.

Wedge-tailed shearwaters return to land in March at the beginning of the nesting season. Adults dig a burrow into sand or soil. They do this by lying on their sides and scraping away the ground with their feet and bills. In places where the ground is too hard or dry to make burrows, they nest in crevices or beneath clumps of grass.

Early in the nesting season before the female lays her egg, pairs of adults sit together in their burrow and make soft moaning sounds to each other. In the evening as more birds return to the colony after sunset, the strange moaning noises grow louder. These sounds often continue throughout the night. The moaning and wailing noises coming from a colony of nesting wedge-tailed shearwaters can sound very frightening, and have caused many people to think they were hearing ghosts.

The female shearwater lays an egg in June or July. Both parents take turns incubating the egg until it hatches in August. The young birds are usually ready to leave the nest in November.

CHRISTMAS SHEARWATER

The Christmas shearwater is the smallest shearwater in Hawai'i. Its body is gray-brown all over, with a dark bill, dark legs, and a rounded tail. It nests on many of the Northwest Hawaiian Islands and in other parts of the Pacific. Although Christmas shearwaters will use empty burrows or holes to nest in, they will not dig burrows of their own. Instead, they choose to nest in rocky crevices or sandy hollows under bushes.

Adult Christmas shearwaters begin to arrive on land in March. Like wedge-tailed shearwaters, they make interesting moaning calls during the nesting season. Females lay a single egg between April and July. The young birds leave for sea between August and November.

Christmas Shearwaters

Newell's Shearwater, or 'A'o

Newell's shearwaters are black above and white below, with a dark bill and legs. These seabirds probably once nested on most of the high islands of Hawai'i, but pigs, dogs, cats, rats, and mongooses, brought to the islands by people, destroyed most of the colonies. Today, they are known to nest on Kaua'i, the Big Island of Hawai'i, and probably Moloka'i and O'ahu.

In mid-April and May, adult Newell's shearwaters return to their nesting sites high in the mountains. They fly inland after sunset and return to sea before dawn. These pigeon-sized birds are not easily noticed as they pass silently overhead in the dark. But when one calls out in flight, its voice is unmistakable: a harsh, rasping "hee-haw, hee-haw, hee-haw."

Newell's shearwaters nest in burrows which they dig into the mountain slopes, often beneath thick layers of ferns. Because their nesting colonies are few and difficult for scientists to reach, little is known about the chicks. Newell's shearwaters lay their single egg in early June, and the egg probably hatches between mid-July and August. By early October, most of the parents have returned to sea for the rest of the year, leaving the chicks on their own.

Each chick leaves the burrow when it feels ready. It has never seen

Newell's Shearwater

the sea, but it takes flight at night, using its instinct to lead it to the sea and guide it to food. Most chicks leave the nest in October or November. As they fly from their mountain burrows to the sea they cross over towns and highways, and are often confused by lights. Many Newell's shearwaters are injured, killed, or just brought down to earth when they become confused and run into objects. Many also "trip" on high power lines that run across their path of flight between mountains and sea. Even if a shearwater is not injured after its fall, it cannot take flight from flat ground. On Kaua'i, a rescue program called Save Our Shearwaters (S.O.S.) picks up hundreds of fallen Newell's shearwaters each year. People in the community find the fallen birds and bring them to rescue stations around the island where they are checked for injuries and, if they are healthy, set free.

STORM-PETRELS

Storm-petrels are the smallest seabirds in the world. They fly close to the water, and during storms they find protection from the wind in the dips between large waves, or along the sides of ships at sea. Hawai'i's storm-petrels feed far out at sea. They feed mostly at night, using their attraction to light and their good sense of smell to help them find small food animals near the surface of the ocean. Storm-petrels fly almost like butterflies as they feed, touching the water lightly without landing. While fluttering their wings, their webbed feet "patter" along the sea surface, almost walking on water as they fly.

The nesting behavior of storm-petrels is similar to other petrels and shearwaters. They nest in burrows or crevices and go to and from their nesting areas at night. The female lays a single white egg at the end of the burrow and both parents incubate it until it hatches. Parents feed the new chick food from their stomachs about once a day at first, but less and less often as the chick grows older. When the chick is ready, it leaves the burrow alone at night and heads to sea.

Band-rumped Storm-Petrel

Sooty Storm-Petrel

BAND-RUMPED STORM-PETREL OR ʻAKĒʻAKĒ

Band-rumped storm-petrels, also called Hawaiian storm-petrels and Harcourt's storm-petrels, are the smallest seabirds in Hawaiʻi. They have dark gray-brown bodies with a white band across the rump and a pale brown bar on each wing. These birds nest in the Galapagos Islands and Japan, as well as on Kauaʻi and Hawaiʻi. They are very rare and quite vulnerable to predation by mammals.

SOOTY STORM-PETREL

Sooty storm-petrels, also called Tristram storm-petrels, are large grayish-brown with pale brown wing bars and long, forked tails. They nest in the Northwest Hawaiian Islands and some islands farther north. Sooty storm-petrels are around the islands during the nesting season, from October through June.

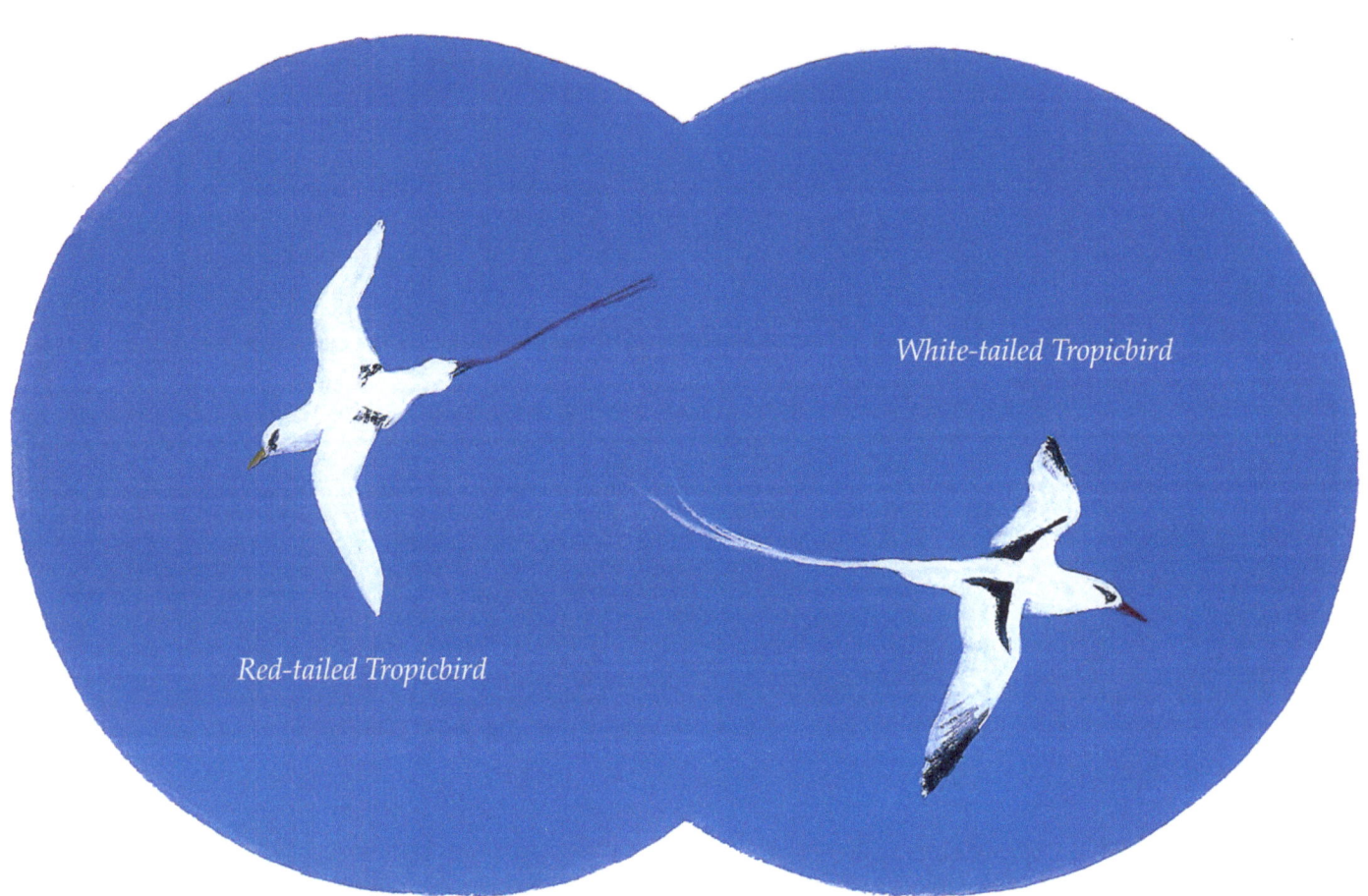

Tropicbirds

Two species of tropicbird nest in Hawai'i: the white-tailed tropicbird, and the red-tailed tropicbird. While white-tailed tropicbirds live throughout the warm oceans of the world, red-tailed tropicbirds live only in warm areas of the Pacific and Indian Oceans. When they see a fish as they are flying, tropicbirds fold their wings and dive into the water to catch it. Sacks of air under the skin protect the neck as they hit the water. Tropicbirds have legs that are set so far back on their bodies that they cannot stand and walk, but their strong wings can lift them easily from the ground without the help of wind.

Female tropicbirds lay a single purplish, speckled egg. Both parents take turns incubating the egg for about 43 days until it hatches. Parents feed the new chick regurgitated food every day, feeding the chick less often as it grows older. As with other seabirds, the chick grows heavier than the parents, but loses the extra weight as it begins to grow feathers and exercise its wings. Although young tropicbirds stay near the island for the first several weeks after leaving the nest, they are not fed by their parents after they learn to fly.

Tropicbirds begin to nest when they are four years old, and are known to live at least twenty eight years.

WHITE-TAILED TROPICBIRD

White-tailed tropicbirds are mostly white with a black stripe through each eye and black across the wings and back. They have two very long, white, tail feathers called *streamers*. Immature birds have black stripes on their backs.

Hawai'i's white-tailed tropicbirds nest in rocky cliffs on Hawai'i, Maui, Lana'i, O'ahu, and Kaua'i. They can often be seen flying around their nests in cliffs and canyons far from the ocean.

Nesting season begins in the spring but some birds may be found nesting at any time of year. Unlike many seabirds that disappear from the islands when they are not nesting, white-tailed tropicbirds stay near the islands all year.

Tropicbirds court each other in the air. Courting pairs of white-tailed tropicbirds can be seen flying next to each other along the cliffs, calling back and forth. The male flies above the female and brushes her from time to time with his long tail streamers.

RED-TAILED TROPICBIRD

Red-tailed tropicbirds are mostly white with a red bill, black stripes through the eyes, and two long, red, tail feathers. Red-tailed tropicbirds nest on some of the Northwestern Hawaiian Islands, in small parts of Ni'ihau, Kaua'i, and Lana'i, and on small islands off of O'ahu and Moloka'i.

Usually, red-tailed tropicbirds nest along the coast. They make a hollowed out nest in sand or soil under shrubs or clumps of grass, or occasionally in caves and under overhanging rocks. Their main nesting season is from March through November.

Males and females court each other in the air. As one bird makes a long, low glide, the other bird flaps its wings and climbs higher in the air while the wind blows it backwards. Then, as the first bird climbs higher in the air, while flapping its wings and letting the wind blow it backwards, the second bird begins a low glide. To someone who is watching from the ground, it looks as if the two birds are taking turns flying in backwards circles.

Red-footed Booby

BOOBIES

Boobies live in tropical oceans throughout the world. They feed on fish and squid, and are often seen flying around ships. They like to catch flying fish that leap from the waves in front of ships, and they sometimes feed on fish scraps and garbage thrown overboard. Often, boobies can be seen sitting on dock pilings or on objects floating at sea. A feeding booby first catches sight of its food as it flies, then folds its wings and dives into the ocean. The nostrils can close to keep out sea water, and air sacs beneath the skin of the throat protect the neck as the bird slams into the ocean. Boobies can dive to a depth of about 5 meters (about 16 feet).

Like frigatebirds, immature boobies wander hundreds of miles, while adult boobies remain nearer to their nesting colonies. Adult boobies sleep on shore throughout the year. Boobies may nest in any month of the year, but most begin nesting during spring and summer. Most boobies start nesting at about 4 years old, and many of them keep the same mate year after year. They recognize each other by sight and sound (the male's voice is higher than the female's). Boobies are known to live at least twenty to twenty-five years.

Although most birds incubate their eggs by sitting with the egg against their breast, boobies do it dif-

Masked Booby

ferently. They wrap their webbed feet over the egg while sitting with their body weight on the outer toes. Males and females take turns sitting on the egg.

When the chick hatches, after about six weeks, the parents put the chick on top of their feet and sit gently over it. Within several days the chick's eyes open, and in a week the chick's body is covered with a thin white fuzz, called *down*. In three weeks the chick has a thick covering of down.

By seven weeks the chick's feathers are growing and it weighs a little more than its parents. As the feathers continue to grow and the young bird starts flapping its wings to build its muscles for flying, the chick begins to lose weight. After three or four months, the chick is ready to fly. Parents continue to feed their chick for one or two months after the young bird leaves the nest. During this time, the young booby learns to catch food for itself.

Three species of booby nest in Hawai'i: the brown booby, the red-footed booby, and the masked booby.

Brown Booby

Brown Booby

Red-footed Booby

Brown Booby or 'Ā

The brown booby has a dark brown head, back, and neck, with a white breast and belly. The undersides of the wings are white with brown edges. Males and females look alike, but during the breeding season the male's feet, face, and bill become more bluish, while the female's feet, face, and bill become more yellow-green. Immature birds look similar to adults.

Unlike masked and red-footed boobies, brown boobies feed on smaller fish near shore. They stay within sight of land and eat alone or among flocks of other seabirds.

Brown boobies often choose nesting spots that overlook a drop-off so they can take flight more easily. They scrape a shallow depression in the ground, often near clumps of grass or shrubs, and line it with twigs and grass. Like the masked booby, the female brown booby usually lays two eggs, but only one chick survives.

Red-footed Booby or 'Ā

The red-footed booby is the smallest of Hawai'i's boobies. It has a white body and yellowish-white head, with black along the outer edges of the wings. The bill is blue with a pink base. The skin on the face is pink, and the legs and feet are bright red. Immature birds look similar to brown boobies during their first two years. A few adults remain brown all over, or brown with a lighter head and white tail.

Red-footed boobies feed far out at sea. They don't feed together, but may join flocks of other seabirds feeding over a school of fish. Red-footed boo-

bies have larger eyes than the other boobies, and they can see better at night. Because of this, they are more active during dark hours, and often nap on land at their colony during the day.

Unlike other Hawaiian boobies, the webbed feet of Red-footed boobies can grip branches, allowing them to sleep in trees at night, and to build their nests on top of shrubs or low trees.

Both red-footed boobies and great frigatebirds choose similar nesting sites and often nest near each other. Unlike masked and brown boobies, red-footed boobies lay only one egg.

Masked Booby or 'Ā

The masked booby, also called blue-faced booby or white booby, is the largest of Hawai'i's boobies. Adult birds are white with black along the outer edges of the wings and tail. They have yellow bills, dark gray or black skin around the eyes and bill, and grayish-green legs and feet. Males and females look alike, but during the breeding season, the male's bill becomes brighter yellow. Immature masked boobies look similar to brown boobies during their first year, and become speckled with white during their second year. By their third year, the brown feathers have been replaced by white, and they look like adults.

Masked boobies nest on sandy or rocky ground. The male clears away pebbles and twigs to make a bare circular area on the ground. This is the "nest." The female usually lays two eggs, but if both eggs hatch the stronger chick kills the weaker one.

FRIGATEBIRDS

Frigatebirds live in warm oceans around the world. They are easily recognized by their large black form, their long, slim, wings and deeply forked tail, as they soar like kites above the sea. The deeply forked tail is often closed in flight.

Frigatebirds do not dive or sit on the ocean's surface because their wings are so long and their legs so small and weak that they cannot take flight from the water. They feed by snatching their food - usually fish and squid - from the surface of the sea as they fly by.

Frigatebird parents catch mostly fish and squid to feed their chicks, but they will also eat baby sea turtles and seabird chicks.

Frigatebirds are great robbers. They steal sticks and even chicks from each other's nests, and they steal food from other seabirds, especially boobies. They sometimes chase a bird until it drops a fish it is carrying, or until it regurgitates food it has already swallowed.

Frigatebirds feed during the day and sleep at night. They may either sleep in trees or shrubs on shore, or sleep while soaring high over the ocean. Although young birds may live at sea and wander long distances away from land, once they are old enough to nest they remain near their nesting colonies throughout the year.

Male

Female

juvenile

Great Frigatebirds

Male with inflated gular pouch

More than any other seabird, frigatebirds are built for flying. They are skilled and graceful in the air, but they can hardly walk or swim. Frigatebirds use their weak legs and feet only to perch in trees or shrubs.

GREAT FRIGATEBIRD, OR 'IWA

The great frigatebird is the only frigatebird that nests in Hawai'i. Adult male great frigatebirds are glossy black, while adult females are black with a white throat and breast. Immature birds - those which are not yet adults - have heads, throats, and breasts of white mixed with some rust color.

Great frigatebirds nest on most of the Northwestern Hawaiian Islands. The birds are seven to eleven years old when they begin to nest. Males have a sack of orange skin at the throat, called a *gular pouch*, which is not usually very noticeable. At the start of the nesting season, from January through April, this skin turns bright red. To attract a female to his nesting site, the male frigatebird fills this pouch full of air, like a red balloon. Then he points his bill to the sky, spreads his wings, and shakes his head back and forth while making chattering noises. If a female is impressed, she lands beside him, choosing him as her mate for the nesting season. Great frigatebirds build a flat nest of twigs and branches that is usually placed on low bushes.

Once the single egg is laid, between January and June, the parents take turns *incubating*, or sitting on it. After about 55 days a naked chick with purplish-gray skin hatches from the egg. The chick is weak and helpless, and for the first month one parent or the other must stay with the young bird and shade it from sun, keep it warm, and protect it from other frigatebirds who might eat it.

Chicks begin to take their first flights from September through November. Because it takes frigatebirds a long time to learn how to catch food for themselves, the parents may continue to feed the young bird for a year or more after it has learned to fly. Great frigatebirds live at least 30 and perhaps as long as 50 years.

TERNS AND NODDIES

Six species of terns and noddies nest in the Hawaiian Islands. Noddies are also terns. They have been given the name noddy because they bow and nod their heads as they court each other. Terns and noddies are slim birds with long, pointed wings and straight, thin bills. Although they all have webbed feet, most terns and noddies spend very little time sitting on the water and only the brown noddy can swim.

Terns and noddies are often seen feeding in flocks, hovering in mid-air above a school of fish, then dropping suddenly to the surface to grab their prey with their pointed bills. They catch fish and squid at the surface after the fish or squid have been chased there by larger fish such as tuna. Fishermen look for flocks of feeding terns, knowing that in the ocean beneath the birds they will find schools of tuna or dolphin fish.

Most terns and noddies nest in spring and summer, but nests can be found throughout the year. Females lay a single egg and will lay another egg to replace it if the first one is lost. By the time the chick is about three weeks old, the parents spend most of their time at sea seeking food. The chicks continue to be fed by their parents for as long as several months after they learn to fly.

Sooty Tern

Sooty Tern or 'Ewa'Ewa

Sooty terns have a black cap and black stripe through each eye, separating the white v-shape on the forehead from their white front and underparts. The upper parts of their wings, back, and tail are black, and the tail is deeply forked. There are more sooty terns in the tropical Pacific Ocean than any other species of seabird, and they nest throughout the tropics. In Hawai'i, they nest in the Northwestern Hawaiian Islands and on some small islands off O'ahu.

Sooty terns nest in dense colonies of up to two million birds. The nesting season varies from place to place and year to year, but adult birds usually arrive on the islands in February, and the female lays one speckled egg between March and May. By September, the chicks are grown and all the birds head back to sea until the following year.

Sooty terns nest close together on open sandy or rocky ground. The air is often filled with terns flying over the colony screeching in high, harsh voices. Both parents incubate the egg for about a month until it hatches. Parents protect the new chick for the first eight days or so. Once the chick is old enough to be left alone it hides among rocks or beneath clumps of grass. Chicks often group together as they hide in the shade. This is an important way for chicks to find shelter from the hot sun. Adults feed their chick by regurgitating food which the chick takes from the parent's mouth. Often parents returning from sea are surrounded by chicks begging to be fed. Parents learn to recognize their own chick's voice. They feed only their own chick, and peck at other chicks that come too near.

Sooty tern chicks fly from the nest at about eight weeks and remain away during the day, but return at night to be fed by their parents.

GRAY-BACKED TERN OR *PĀKALAKALA*

Gray-backed terns, also called Spectacled Terns, have a black cap and black stripe through each eye, separating the white v-shape on the forehead from the white front and under-parts. They look similar to sooty terns but the white v-shape on the gray-back's forehead is longer than the sooty's, and the gray-back's feathers on its back, wings, and deeply forked tail are gray instead of black. The legs, feet, and bill are black.

In Hawai'i, gray-backed terns nest in the Northwest Chain and on small islands off O'ahu. They are much less common than sooty terns. Adults usually return to the islands to nest in January or February and lay their eggs just before the sooty terns do. The single, speckled egg is laid on sand or hard ground, sometimes under plants or in hollows on lava rock. Like sooty terns, gray-backed tern chicks group together in the shade to keep cool.

White (Fairy) Tern

WHITE TERN OR *MANU-O-KŪ*

The white tern, also called fairy tern, is a snowy white bird with a black ring around its eye, and a black bill with a blue base. The legs and feet are gray with white webs and the tail is slightly forked.

White terns nest throughout the tropical Pacific and on the Northwestern Hawaiian Islands. Since 1961, they have also been seen nesting on Oʻahu. Most white terns nest between April and June, but eggs can be found throughout the year. No nest is made at all. The female lays an egg on the branch of a tree or bush, or on rocks or man-made objects - any place that is above the surrounding ground. Parents take turns incubating the egg for about 35 days until it hatches. The newly hatched chick has long toes and claws that can grip the branch and hold on tight. Because white terns lay their eggs in places where the egg can fall easily, many eggs are lost each year.

White terns dive to the surface of the water to catch small fish, which they carry crosswise in their bills. One bird can carry many little fish in its bill, all in a row, as it brings them to the nest to feed its chick. The chick takes each fish, one at a time, from the parent's bill and swallows it. The young tern can fly after about 45 days, but at first it stays near the nest site. It continues to be fed by its parents for two to four months after it can fly.

NODDIES

Noddy terns, also called *noddies*, are named after their habit of nodding and bowing during courtship. They nest throughout the Pacific, and in Hawai'i they can be found nesting in the Northwest Chain and on small islands off the main islands. Noddies have been found nesting on some islands at any time of the year, but most birds nest in winter and spring.

BLACK NODDY OR *NOIO*

The black noddy is dark with a white cap and white ring below the eye, a long pointed bill, and a forked tail. On some birds, the white cap turns gradually into dark gray-brown on the back and undersides while the rump is pale gray and the tail is dark gray. Other birds are dark gray-black all over with a white cap. The bill and feet are black. These birds are less common than brown noddies, but they are found nesting on islands throughout the tropical Pacific. In Hawai'i, they nest in the Northwest Chain and along the coasts and small islands off the main islands. Black noddies sleep on shore at night throughout the year.

Black noddies can be found nesting in some places at any time of the year, but the main nesting season is from winter to spring, with most eggs laid in December and January.

Black Noddy

Brown Noddy

NODDIES

Blue-gray Noddy

Black noddies nest in bushes, trees, on rock ledges or in crevices, and even in cliff holes. Nests are built of grass, twigs, leaves, and seaweed. The female lays a single egg with scattered markings on it. Newly hatched chicks are black with a whitish cap, or sometimes gray all over. The chicks are ready to fly at about 38 days old.

BROWN NODDY OR *NOIO KŌHĀ*

The brown noddy has a chocolate brown body with a whitish cap on the head. The tail is wedge-shaped and the legs and bill are black. The eyes have a white rim along the underside.

Brown noddies can nest on the ground, in shrubs, or on ledges. Brown noddy chicks hatch with a covering of down that may be black, gray, or white. Noddy chicks are ready to leave the nest at about 42 days old. Although they leave the nest during the day, they return in the afternoon to be fed by their parents for another three months or so.

BLUE-GRAY NODDY

The blue-gray noddy, also called Necker Island tern, is the smallest tern in the world. It is bluish gray with a short black bill and a white ring below the eye. It has a slightly forked tail and black feet with yellow webs between the toes. Some birds have pale faces and under-parts; others do not.

Blue-gray noddies roost on shore all year and stay fairly near the islands when feeding. They nest throughout parts of the Pacific, and on some of the Northwestern Hawaiian Islands. The female lays a single egg with scattered markings in a shallow hole in rocks or cliffs, or on sand beneath low shrubs. Most eggs are laid between December and mid-March, and the chicks leave the nest by mid-May.

A frigatebird drops its wings and head, allowing more air to blow across the surface of its body.

Surviving the Heat

Parent birds and their chicks spend many long weeks on land during the nesting season, and Hawai'i's weather is often hot. While shearwaters and petrels avoid the heat by nesting in burrows and coming ashore at night, many other seabirds nest on very hot ground and in very strong sunlight. These birds must have ways to keep cool, or they will die.

Adult seabirds use their bodies to shade their egg and young chick from the sun, but adult birds and older chicks must keep cool in other ways. The adults and older chicks of albatrosses, terns, and noddies keep cool by panting quickly with their bills open. Moisture inside the mouth provides cooling by water loss, like a dog panting on a hot day. Albatross adults and chicks also cool themselves by sit-

A tern chick pants like a dog to keep cool.

ting back on their heels with their toes in the air. The webbed skin of their feet contains many blood vessels. The blood in the feet gets cooled as the breeze passes by the toes. Older albatross chicks and tern chicks also cool themselves by finding a shady spot to sit in during the day.

While albatrosses, terns, and noddies pant to keep cool, frigatebirds and boobies also flutter their throats. Fluttering the soft skin at the bottom of the mouth provides cooling by water loss, and takes less effort than panting. Frigatebirds and boobies sometimes droop their wings and heads in the heat. This allows more of the body's surface area to be touched by cooling breezes.

Many seabirds keep cool by sitting or standing with their backs to the sun and raising the feathers along the back. This keeps their face and feet - parts which aren't well protected by feathers - in the shade, while the raised back feathers allow cool air to move near the skin.

A booby keeps cool by fluttering the skin at its throat.

An albatross chick keeps cool by allowing the breeze to blow on its feet.

Sun, wind, rain, and high seas take the lives of some seabirds each year.

OTHER DANGERS

Hawai'i's seabirds face many dangers on land besides the hot sun. Nesting birds may lose chicks and eggs during high winds and rainstorms. Some seabird eggs never hatch because the chick never formed inside the egg. Since chicks are fed by both parents, a chick will starve to death if one parent dies, or if the parents can't find enough food that year. Predatory birds such as black-crowned night herons, cattle egrets, and especially great frigatebirds, eat seabird chicks.

One of the main threats to Hawai'i's seabirds that nest on or near the ground comes from *introduced species* - foreign animals that were brought to Hawai'i by people, either on purpose or by accident. Mongooses, cats, and several kinds of rats are introduced species that have killed and eaten so many chicks that they've caused entire colonies of seabirds to disappear from some Hawaiian islands. Dogs, too, are responsible for killing many seabirds at their nesting sites. Mosquitoes are an introduced species that came to Hawai'i by accident in ship's drinking water. Mosquitoes can spread a disease called avian pox that affects some seabirds and can kill chicks.

The ancient Hawaiians ate many seabird eggs and chicks, and today people still eat seabird eggs and chicks in many parts of the world. In the past, feather hunting, egg collecting, and dropping bombs killed many of Hawai'i's nesting seabirds. But in Hawai'i today, biologists and tourists are more likely to kill seabirds without meaning to. People who come close to nesting colonies of seabirds can scare the parent birds away from the nest, causing them to leave an egg or young chick that they were protecting. The unprotected egg or chick may die from too much sun, or be quickly eaten by a frigatebird. Often the egg falls from the nest when a frightened parent leaves the nest suddenly. When frightened sooty tern chicks run too far from their nests they may get lost and be pecked to death by other terns. Bright lights and electrical power lines are a problem for certain seabirds that fly at night, and cause many bird deaths each year. These deaths can be avoided by shielding lights and placing power lines

Large nets designed to catch fish also catch seabirds.

underground along major *flyways*, or paths of flight.

Seabirds face many dangers at sea. High winds and rough seas may kill birds and make it difficult to find food. Sharks and other large fish eat seabirds, and activities by people have brought new problems. Some birds depend on large fish, such as tuna and *mahimahi*, or dolphin fish, to chase small food fish to the surface. Fishing for tuna and *mahimahi* with nets and long-lines has become big business all over the world. Nets, and especially long-lines, used to catch these fish also catch and drown huge numbers of seabirds every year. Businesses that catch small "bait fish" such as herrings, anchovies, young goatfish, and mackerel scad, are taking the same food that seabirds eat. We must be sure that there are enough food fish left in the sea for us all to share.

Other dangers to seabirds come from garbage, chemicals, and oil spills. For years, people have used the oceans as a dumping ground for garbage and poisonous wastes. As we fill the oceans with these wastes, including plastics and chemicals, it is not surprising that they affect all life, including seabirds. Seabirds in Hawai'i and throughout the world have been found with plastic in their stomachs. Parents often feed the plastic to their chicks along with real food. Fortunately, Hawai'i's seabirds do not have large amounts of poisonous chemicals and metals in their bodies, as some birds do in other places. Oil spills are a serious hazard to seabirds because oil on feathers destroys the waxy substance that keeps the feathers water-repellent. Furthermore, as the bird tries to clean the oil from its feathers with its bill, some of the toxic oil is swallowed.

Rats and mongooses can enter underground burrows to reach seabirds and their eggs.

Shearwater

Petrel

Frigatebird

Tropicbird

Storm-petrel

THE FUTURE OF SEABIRDS

Throughout time, Hawai'i's seabirds have been affected by changes in nature such as storms and shifting food supplies. Changes caused by people have come quickly to Hawai'i in recent years. City lights brighten the night sky and electrical power lines run like nets along the shorelines of some islands. Ships and shoreline activities cause oil, plastics and other pollution to enter the ocean. The list of changes is very long. Often, people do not know how much damage a new project will cause to seabirds until the damage has been done. Learning to avoid damage before it happens, and correcting damage that has been done takes desire, time, energy, and money. Above all, it takes an awareness that we must treat all of nature, including seabirds and other people, in the same way that we wish to treat ourselves - with respect, understanding, and loving kindness.

Tern
Noddy

Booby

Albatross

How You Can Help

- **DO** clean up garbage and old fishing nets that you find along the beach.

- **DON'T** throw plastic or other garbage into the sea.

- **DO** learn about public issues concerning seabirds, such as long-line fishing, and lights and power lines that are near seabird flyways.

- **DON'T** disturb seabirds that are sitting on their nests.

- **DO** keep your cats and dogs indoors or under your control, and get them neutered.

- **DO** call the Conservation Hotline if you find an injured seabird: just dial "O" and ask the operator for "Enterprise 5469."

GLOSSARY

burrow   a hole or tunnel dug into the ground which birds use as a nesting place.

colony   a large number of birds which nest near each other within a small area.

court   to try to attract a bird of the opposite sex for breeding.

down   soft, fluffy feathers that seem almost like a fuzzy coat of fur.

extinct   no longer alive on earth.

flock   a group of birds.

flyway   like "highways in the sky," flyways are routes along which many birds fly.

gular pouch   a sack or pouch in the throat which can expand with air.

hover   to flap the wings quickly in mid-air so as to remain almost in one spot.

immature   a young bird which is not yet an adult.

incubate   to sit on eggs to keep them warm so baby birds will grow inside the eggs and hatch.

instinct   knowledge or a behavior pattern that a bird is born with.

introduced species   plants or animals that have been brought to Hawai'i by people.

mammals   any members of the group of animals that feed their young with milk, such as cats, mice, and humans.

perch   to sit on something above the ground, such as a branch.

predator, (predatory, predation)   an animal that hunts other animals for food.

regurgitate   to bring food up from the stomach through the mouth.

school   a group of fish, or other water animals, that swim together.

species   plants or animals of the same kind that are able to breed with one another.

survive   to remain alive.

INDEX

'ā 28, 29
'ake'ake 23
albatross 6, 8, 14, 38, 39
    Laysan 7, 9, 10, 12, 13
    black-footed 10
    short-tailed 10
'a'o 20
avian pox 40
baitfish industry 41
black-crowned night heron 40
booby 6, 7, 26, 27, 30, 39, 43
    masked 27, 28, 29
    brown 27, 28, 29
    red-footed 3, 26, 27, 28, 29
cats 4, 20, 40, 43
cattle egret 40
Conservation Hotline 43
dogs 4, 20, 40, 43
electrical power lines 40, 42
'ewa'ewa 33
feather hunting 10, 40
frigatebirds 6, 26, 30, 38, 39, 42
    great 3, 29, 31, 40
introduced species 40, 44
'iwa 31
Ka'ena Point 12
Ka'ula 5
koa'e 'ula 25
koa'e kea 25
lights, danger from 40
long-line fishing 43
mahimahi fishing 41
Manana 5
manu-o-kū 35
Moku Manu 5, 12
mōli 12
mongoose 4, 16, 20, 40
mosquitoes 40
noddy 32, 36, 38, 39, 43
    brown 32, 36, 37
    black 36, 37
    blue-gray 37
noio 36
noio kōhā 37
oil spills 41
'ou 17
pākalakala 34
petrel 14, 15, 38, 42
    dark-rumped 15, 16
    Bonin 17
    Bulwer's 17
plastics 41, 42
pollution 41, 42
rats 4, 16, 20, 40
Save Our Shearwaters Program 22
sharks 41
shearwater 7, 14, 15, 38, 42
    wedge-tailed 18, 19
    Christmas 19
    Newell's 5, 15, 20, 21
stomach oil 11
storm-petrel 22, 42
    band-rumped 23
    hawaiian 23
    sooty 23
    tristram 23
terns 32, 38, 39, 43
    sooty 3, 6, 32, 33, 34, 40
    gray-backed 34
    white 35
    fairy 35
    Necker Island 37
    spectacled 34
tropicbird 7, 24, 42
    white-tailed 24, 25
    red-tailed 7, 24, 25
tubenoses 14
tuna fishing 41
'ua'u 16
'ua'u kani 18

www.ingramcontent.com/pod-product-compliance
Lightning Source LLC
Chambersburg PA
CBHW042252100526
44587CB00002B/116